Nelson
English

Workbook
Starter B

This book belongs to:

_____

Heather French

OXFORD
UNIVERSITY PRESS

Great Clarendon Street, Oxford, OX2 6DP, United Kingdom

Oxford University Press is a department of the University of Oxford. It furthers the University's objective of excellence in research, scholarship, and education by publishing worldwide. Oxford is a registered trade mark of Oxford University Press in the UK and in certain other countries

Text © Oxford University Press, 2019

Illustrations © Oxford University Press, 2019

British Library Cataloguing in Publication Data

Data available

ISBN: 978-019-844503-6

3 5 7 9 10 8 6 4 2

Paper used in the production of this book is a natural, recyclable product made from wood grown in sustainable forests. The manufacturing process conforms to the environmental regulations of the country of origin.

Printed in India by Manipal Technologies Limited

Acknowledgements
Cover illustration and inside illustrations by Martyn Cain, Beehive Illustration
Page make-up by Q2A Media Services Inc.

Contents

Clothes, Clothes, Clothes!

Phonics and Spelling

j and v

A
1 Find things in the picture that begin with **j**.
2 Find things in the picture that begin with **v**.

B Circle the words you can read.
Read the words aloud.

vest	jog	vet	jam	jet	van	Jack

C
1 Tick the pictures that have a **j** at the **beginning** of the word.
2 Cross the pictures that have a **v** at the **beginning** of the word.

j and v

A **1** Trace the letter **j** with your finger.

 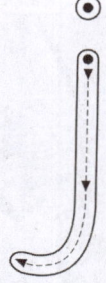 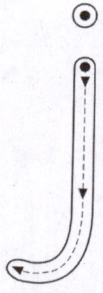 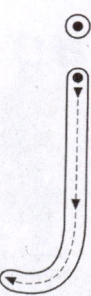

2 Trace the letter **v** with your finger.

B Trace and copy the letters.

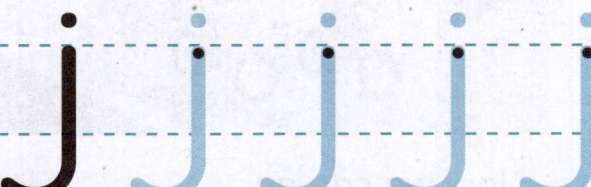

C Complete the words.

_____ t   _____ g   _____ n   _____ t

How did you feel about the activities?
Colour one of the faces.

Comprehension

Outdoor clothes

A Look at the pictures and tell your partner the story.

1

I need my jacket.

2

Jack, you forgot your gloves and scarf.

3

Val, you forgot your helmet and hi-vis vest.

4

Now we can go.

B 1 What did Jack forget?

2 What did Val forget?

C How do some clothes help to keep Jack and Val safe?

Vocabulary

Clothing words

A Match the pictures with the correct labels.

1

2

3

socks   hat   jumper

B Tick the clothes you wear when it is cold.

Grammar and Punctuation

Describing words

pink

blue

brown

purple

orange

green

A 1 Draw a picture of you wearing something in one of the colours above.

2 Write a sentence.

For example: *I like my orange hat.*

B Sing the rhyme.

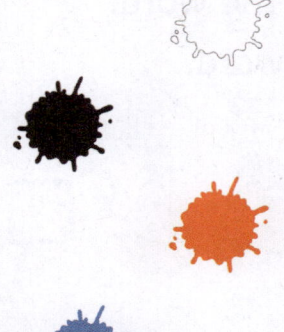

White orange black and blue, black and blue,
White orange black and blue, black and blue,
And purple and green and pink and brown,
White orange black and blue, black and blue.

How did you feel about the activities?
Colour one of the faces.

7

Machines that Help Us

Phonics and Spelling

w and x

A 1 Find things in the picture that begin with **w**.

2 Find things in the picture that begin or end with **x**.

B Circle the words you can read.
Read the words aloud.

| wig | box | wag | six | ox | web | well | went |

C 1 Tick the pictures that have a **w** at the **beginning** of the word.

2 Cross the pictures that have an **x** at the **end** of the word.

Writing

w and x

A **1** Trace the letter **w** with your finger.

 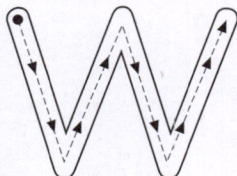 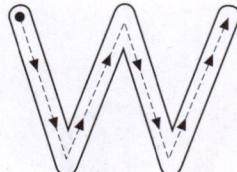 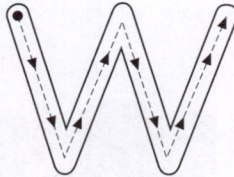

2 Trace the letter **x** with your finger.

 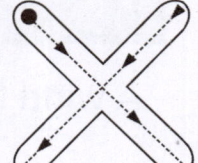 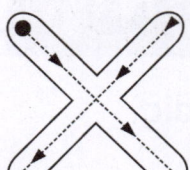 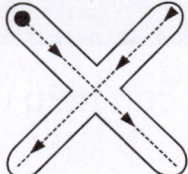

B Trace and copy the letters.

C Complete the words.

___ ___ b   ___ ___ g   f___ ___   b___ ___

How did you feel about the activities?
Colour one of the faces.

Comprehension

Machines we need

A Look at the pictures and tell your partner what you can see.

1

A digger can help us dig.

2

A wind farm gives us power.

3

Machines help us at home.

4

We need machines in hospitals.

B 1 Why do we need wind farms?

    2 How do x-rays help us?

C Which machines do we use at home?

Vocabulary

Machine words

A Match the pictures with the correct labels.

1

2

3

wind farm   x-ray   laptop

B Tick the machines you can find in a house.

[ ]   [ ]   [ ]

[ ]   [ ]   [ ]

Grammar and Punctuation

Doing words

dig   make   type   chat   wash   see   sit   click

A 1 Draw a picture of a machine.

2 Write a sentence to explain how the machine helps us.

For example: *I can dig with a digger.*

B Say the rhyme and do some actions.

If I had a digger, I could dig, dig, dig,
If I had a laptop, I could type, type, type,
If I had a camera, I could click, click, click,
If I had a phone, I could chat, chat, chat,
All day long.

How did you feel about the activities?
Colour one of the faces.

11

Animals Around the World

Phonics and Spelling

y and z

A 1 Find an animal that begins with **y**.
  2 Find an animal that begins with **z**.

B Circle the words you can read.
  Read the words aloud.

zip   yak   zigzag   yes   buzz   zebra   yell   yet

C 1 Tick the pictures that have a **y** at the **beginning** of the word.
  2 Cross the pictures that have a **z** at the **beginning** of the word.

y and z

 1 Trace the letter **y** with your finger.

 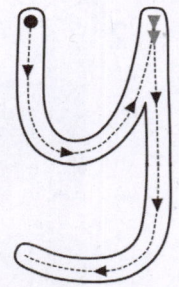 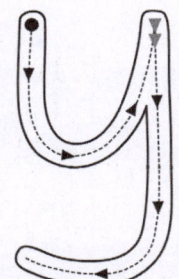 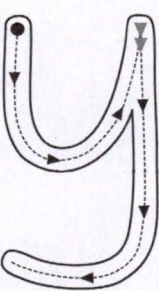

2 Trace the letter **z** with your finger.

 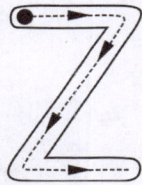 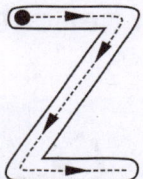 

B Trace and copy the letters.

y y y y y

z z z z z

C Complete the words.

__ __ k __ __ llow __ __ p __ __ __ ra

How did you feel about the activities?
Colour one of the faces.

Comprehension

Animals snapshots

A Look at the pictures and tell your partner what you can see.

1

The polar bear is with her cub.

2

The yaks carry boxes.

3

The zebras are in a herd.

4

The camels walk across the sand.

B 1 How do yaks help the people?

2 Why do you think the men on camels cover their faces?

C What other animals like to be in herds?

Vocabulary

Animal words

A Match the pictures with the correct labels.

1

2

3

camel

parrot

zebra

B **1** Tick the animals that live in a hot place.

2 Cross the animals that live in a cold place.

Grammar and Punctuation

Doing words

lick run jump buzz drink sleep

A **1** Draw a picture of an animal doing something.

2 Write a sentence to say what it can do.

For example: The yak can drink.

B Say the rhyme and do some actions.

The bees can buzz, buzz, buzz,
The parrot can flap, flap, flap,
The zebra can run, run, run,
I can sleep, sleep, sleep,
All day long.

How did you feel about the activities?
Colour one of the faces.

Castles

Phonics and Spelling

th and qu

A 1 Find things in the picture that begin with **th**.

2 Find things in the picture that begin with **qu**.

B Circle the words you can read.
Read the words aloud.

| quilt | thin | quick | quest | thud | quiz | moth | maths |

C 1 Tick the pictures that have **th** at the **beginning** of the word.

2 Cross the pictures that have **qu** at the **beginning** of the word.

th and qu

A **1** Trace the letters **th** with your finger.

 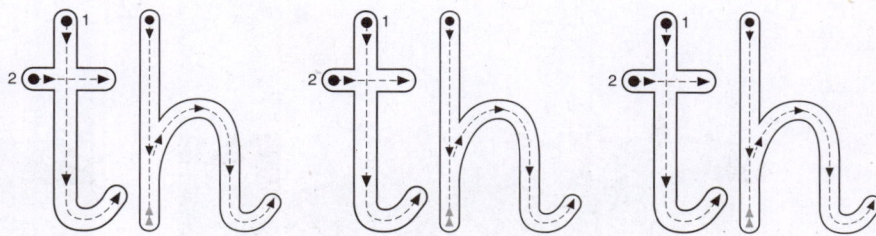

2 Trace the letters **qu** with your finger.

 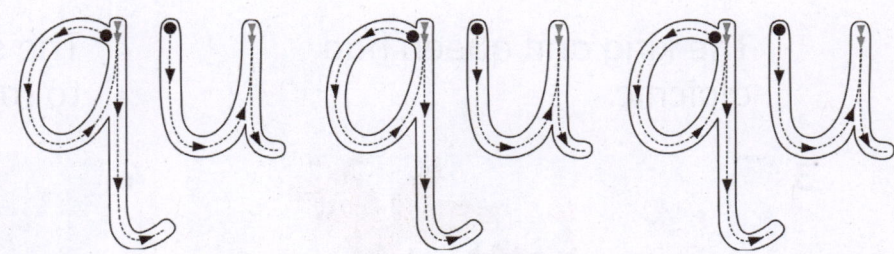

B Trace and copy the letters.

th th th

qu qu qu

C Complete the words.

m _____ _____   b _____ _____ _____ _____ _____   t _____ _____ een

How did you feel about the activities?
Colour one of the faces.

Comprehension

The picnic

A Look at the pictures and tell your partner the story.

1

The king and queen had a picnic.

2

The sun went in. Was it going to rain?

3

Oh no! It's a dragon. Run!

4

You forgot your picnic!

The dragon was kind.

B 1 Who was at the picnic?
   2 Why did they run back into the castle?

C What do you think happened next?

Vocabulary

Castle words

A Match the pictures with the correct labels.

1

2

3

throne   dragon   queen

B **1** Tick the things that would be in a castle.

2 Cross the things that would **not** be in a castle.

 ☐  ☐  ☐

 ☐  ☐  ☐

Grammar and Punctuation

Joining word - and

A **1** Draw a picture of a castle.

2 Write a sentence with the word 'and' in it.

For example: *There is a throne and a king in my castle.*

B Say the rhyme and do some actions.

Castles are big and castles are small,
Castles are short and castles are tall,
Castles have towers up to the sky,
Castles have flags that fly so high,
Castles have queens and castles have kings,
Castles have lots of interesting things.

How did you feel about the activities?
Colour one of the faces.

On the Farm

Phonics and Spelling

sh and ch

A 1 Find an animal that begins with **sh**.
2 Find an animal that begins with **ch**.

B Circle the words you can read.
Read the words aloud.

chip	shell	chin	dish	chop	ship	wish	lunch

C 1 Tick the pictures that have **sh** in the word.
2 Cross the pictures that have **ch** in the word.

sh and ch

A   **1**   Trace the letters **sh** with your finger.

2   Trace the letters **ch** with your finger.

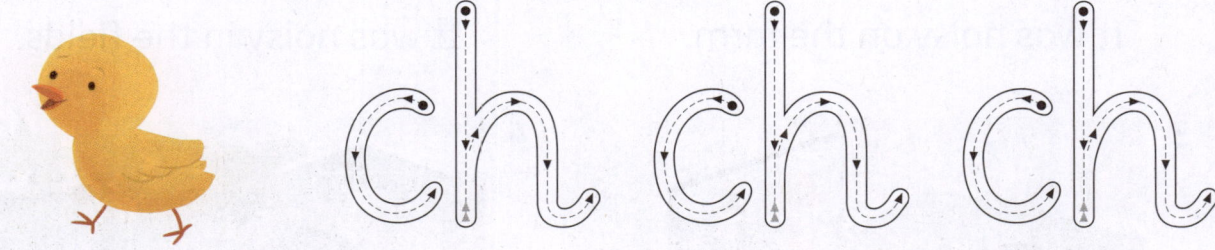

B   Trace and copy the letters.

sh   sh   sh

ch   ch   ch

C   Complete the words.

_____ p   _____ d   _____ n   _____ ck

How did you feel about the activities?
Colour one of the faces.

Comprehension

A problem on the farm

A Look at the pictures and tell your partner the story.

1

It was noisy on the farm.

2

It was noisy in the fields.

3

The man had an idea.

4

That's much better now!

B 1 What was the problem in this story?
2 How was the problem solved?

C Do you like the ending of the story? Why or why not?

Vocabulary

Farm words

A Match the pictures with the correct labels.

1

2

3

duck   chick   sheep

B Tick the animals you would see on a farm.

Grammar and Punctuation

Plurals

A **1** Draw a picture of a farm.

2 Write a sentence about the animals on your farm.

For example: There are ducks and chicks on my farm.

B Sing the song and do some actions.

Old Macdonald had a farm, E-I-E-I-O
And on that farm he had a dog, E-I-E-I-O
With a woof woof here,
And a woof woof there,
Here a woof, there a woof,
Everywhere a woof woof,
Old Macdonald had a farm, E-I-E-I-O.

How did you feel about the activities?
Colour one of the faces.

Phonics and Spelling

ai and ng

A 1 Find these **ai** words in the picture:

> s**ai**l   tr**ai**n   sn**ai**l

2 Find children doing these things in the picture:

> kicki**ng**   jumpi**ng**   runni**ng**   throwi**ng**

B Circle the words you can read.
Read the words aloud.

| pain | song | tail | fang | spring | rain | bang | paint |

C 1 Tick the pictures that have **ai** in the word.
2 Cross the pictures that have **ng** in the word.

ai and ng

 1 Trace the letters **ai** with your finger.

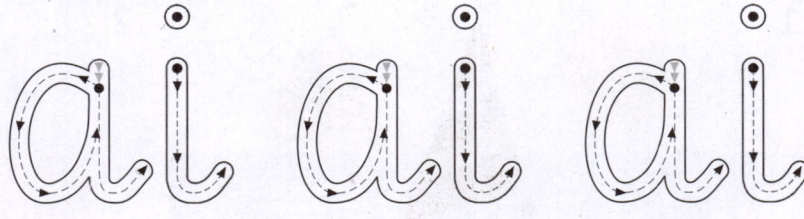

2 Trace the letters **ng** with your finger.

B Trace and copy the letters.

ai *ai ai*

ng *ng ng*

C Complete the words.

w _ _ _ _ _ _ s _ _ _ _ _ p _ _ _ _ _ _ s _ _ _ _ _ _

How did you feel about the activities?
Colour one of the faces.

Comprehension

All sorts of sports

A Look at the pictures and tell your partner what you can see.

1

We like sailing.

2

We like running.

3

We like swimming.

4

We like playing cricket.

B
1 Which sports need water?
2 Which sport has a bat and ball?

C What sport do you like doing?

Vocabulary

Sports words

A Match the pictures with the correct labels.

1

2

3

tennis   swimming   running

B Tick which sports need water.

Grammar and Punctuation

Capital letters and spacing

A 1 Draw a picture of you doing a sport.

  2 Write a sentence.

  For example: *I like running.*

B Say the rhyme and do some actions.

Catch and run,
Spin and throw,
Jumping up and go, go, go.

Spinning round,
Touching toes,
Jumping up and row, row, row.

How did you feel about the activities?
Colour one of the faces.

Water Fun

Phonics and Spelling

oa and ee

A   **1** Find these **oa** words in the picture:

t**oa**d   r**oa**d   b**oa**t

2 Find these **ee** words in the picture:

b**ee**   tr**ee**   **ee**l

B Circle the words you can read.
Read the words aloud.

green   boat   see   coat   sweep   sheet   throat   float

C   **1** Tick the pictures that have **oa** in the word.
2 Cross the pictures that have **ee** in the word.

 ☐    ☐    ☐

 ☐    ☐    ☐

oa and ee

A **1** Trace the letters **oa** with your finger.

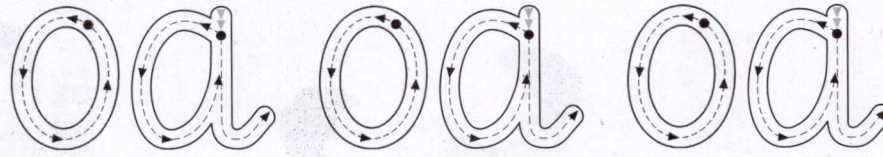

2 Trace the letters **ee** with your finger.

B Trace and copy the letters.

oa oa oa

ee ee ee

C Complete the words.

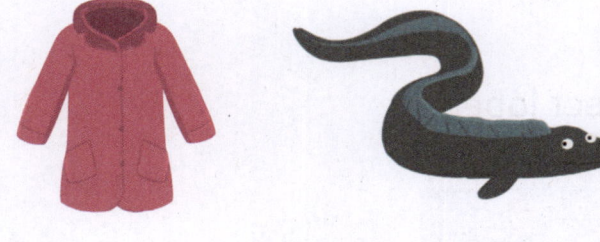

c_____   _____l   t_____   t_____

How did you feel about the activities?
Colour one of the faces.

Comprehension

We need water

A Look at the pictures and tell your partner what you can see.

1

We wash our hands.

2

We have a drink.

3

We wash the car.

4

We play with sand and water.

B 1 What are the children doing in the bathroom?

2 What are the children doing in the kitchen?

C What do you think the children will do with their buckets of water?

Vocabulary

Water words

A Match the pictures with the correct labels.

1

2

3

swim

drink

float

B Tick the pictures that need water.

Grammar and Punctuation

Simple sentences

A 1 Tell your partner when you need water.

2 Write a sentence.

For example: *I need water to brush my teeth.*

B Say the rhyme and do some actions.

Water is for everyone,
It helps our plants to grow.
We need it for our washing,
It even makes the snow.

So do not waste it,
Stop that drip.
Water is good,
Every last sip.

How did you feel about the activities?
Colour one of the faces.

Party Time

Phonics and Spelling

oo and ar

A **1** Find these **oo** words in the picture:

f**oo**d   kangar**oo**   b**oo**k   h**oo**k

2 Find these **ar** words in the picture:

c**ar**d   st**ar**   sh**ar**k   **ar**m

B Circle the words you can read.
Read the words aloud.

cook   bark   cart   look   moon   start   balloon   tart

C **1** Tick the pictures that have **oo** in the word.
2 Cross the pictures that have **ar** in the word.

oo/oo and ar

A **1** Trace the letters **oo** with your finger.

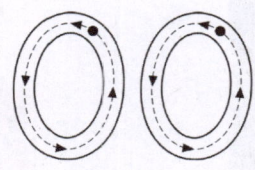 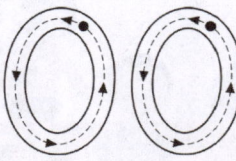 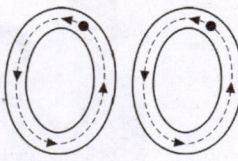

2 Trace the letters **ar** with your finger.

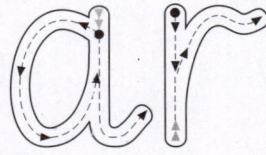 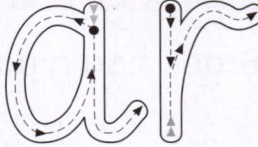 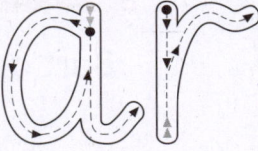

B Trace and copy the letters.

oo oo oo

ar ar ar

C Complete the words.

c _____   m _____   s _____   b _____

How did you feel about the activities?
Colour one of the faces.

Comprehension

The birthday party

A Look at the pictures and tell your partner the story.

1

Bart and Brook had a party.

2

They had fun with balloons.

3

There was lots of party food.

4

They sang a birthday song.

B 1 How old are Bart and Brook?

2 What party food can you see?

C What do you think will happen next at the party?

Vocabulary

Party words

A Draw a picture for these words.

balloon	party hat

B Match the pictures with the correct sentences.

1    I can sing a song.

2    I can make a birthday card.

3    I can blow up a balloon.

Grammar and Punctuation

Simple sentences

 A 1 Tell your partner about a party you have been to.

2 Write a sentence.

For example: *I had fun with balloons.*

B Sing the song.

Change the underlined words and sing it again.

Happy Birthday to you,
Happy Birthday to you,
<u>With popcorn and potatoes</u>,
Happy Birthday to you.

How did you feel about the activities?
Colour one of the faces.

Night and Day

Phonics and Spelling

or and ow

A **1** Find these **or** words in the picture:

> t**or**ch   p**or**ch   st**or**k

2 Find these **ow** words in the picture:

> **ow**l   cl**ow**n   cr**ow**n

B Circle the words you can read.
Read the words aloud.

> for   town   fort   howl   cow   port   growl   sort

C **1** Tick the pictures that have **or** in the word.
2 Cross the pictures that have **ow** in the word.

or and ow

A **1** Trace the letters **or** with your finger.

 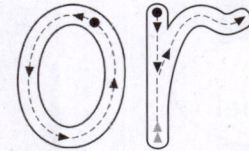 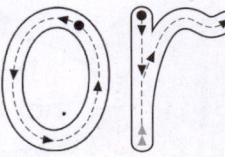 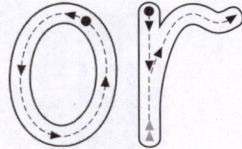

2 Trace the letters **ow** with your finger.

B Trace and copy the letters.

ow ow ow

or or or

C Complete the words.

t_____ch   c_____   c_____   f_____

How did you feel about the activities?
Colour one of the faces.

Comprehension

Lost!

A Look at the pictures and tell your partner the story.

1

It is too hot for me!

It was a hot day.

2

Porsha, Porsha! Come in now!

When it got dark the children went in.

3

Porsha was lost. Where was she?

4

Here she is!

Porsha was in the fort.

B 1 Why did Mum go inside?

2 Who was lost?

C What do you think happened next?

Vocabulary

Night and day words

A Draw a picture for these words.

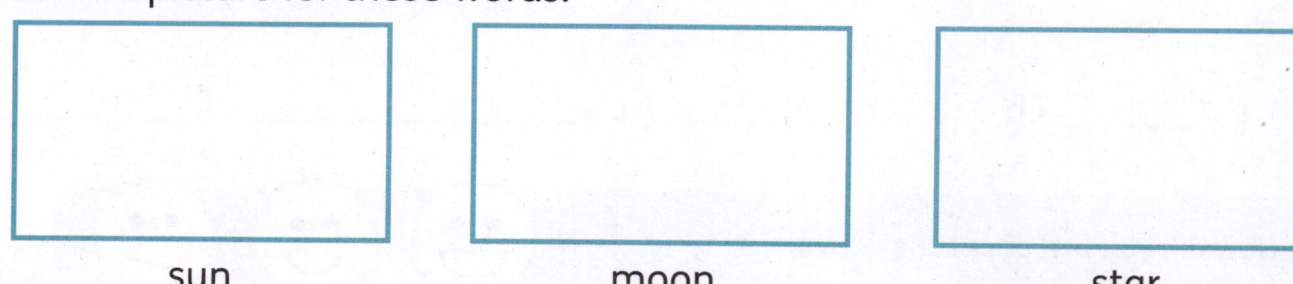

sun   moon   star

B Match the pictures with the correct sentences.

1    This is my crown.

2    I have a torch.

3    I can see an owl.

Grammar and Punctuation

Questions and answers

A 1 Ask your partner questions about bedtime.
When do you go to bed?
What do you do before you go to bed?

2 Write down an answer.
For example: *I brush my teeth.*

B Say the rhyme and do some actions.

The sun is up,
The sun is down,
It shines so brightly on our town.
The moon is up,
The moon is down,
It shines so gently on our town.

How did you feel about the activities?
Colour one of the faces.

Phonics and Spelling

oi and ur

A **1** Find these **oi** words in the picture:

oil c**oi**ns tinf**oi**l

2 Find these **ur** words in the picture:

p**ur**se t**ur**nip t**ur**key

B Circle the words you can read.
Read the words aloud.

fur boil burn hurt join turn spoil point

C **1** Tick the pictures that have **oi** in the word.
2 Cross the pictures that have **ur** in the word.

oi and ur

 A **1** Trace the letters **oi** with your finger.

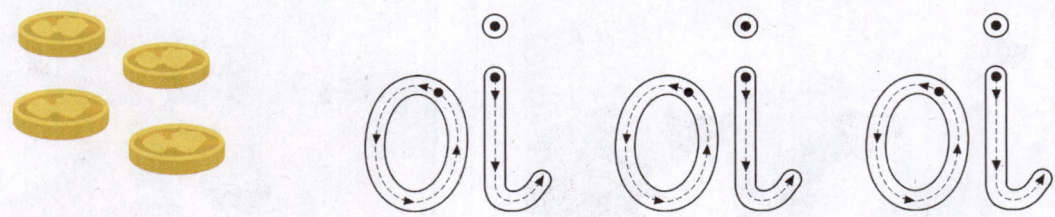

2 Trace the letters **ur** with your finger.

B Trace and copy the letters.

oi oi oi

ur ur ur

C Complete the words.

s_____   c_____   c_____   s t_____

How did you feel about the activities?
Colour one of the faces.

Cooking in different places

A Look at the pictures and tell your partner what you can see.

1

Food is cooked in a kitchen.

2

Food is cooked on a barbecue.

3

Food is cooked in a
tandoor oven.

4

Food is cooked in a
microwave oven.

B 1 What are the cooks doing in the kitchen?

2 What is cooking on the barbecue?

3 Do you think the tandoor oven or microwave cooks food the quickest?

C Have you cooked outside? What did you cook?

Vocabulary

Cookery words

A Draw a picture for these words.

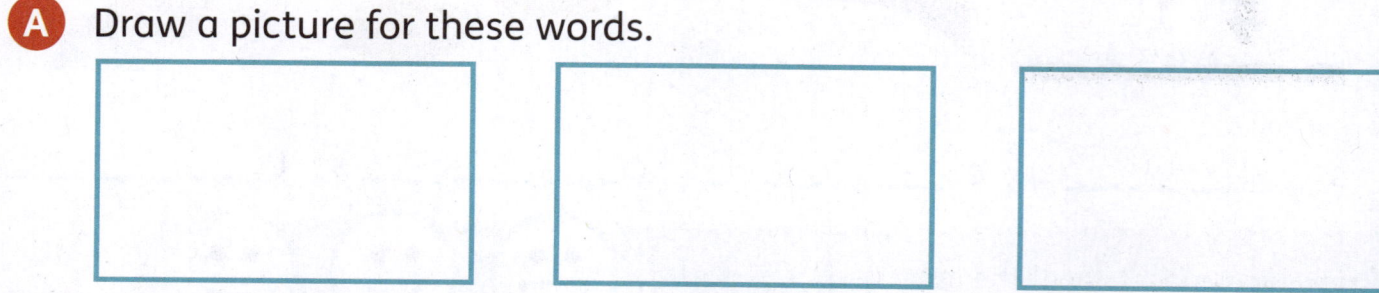

fork   pan   spoon

B Match the pictures with the correct sentences.

1    She is holding a cup.

2    She has burnt the chips.

3    The water is boiling.

Grammar and Punctuation

Writing lists

 A 1 Draw the fruit you would put in a fruit salad.

2 Complete the sentence with a list of fruit.

In my fruit salad, I like _____

B Say the rhyme and do some actions.

Pat-a-cake, pat-a-cake, baker's man,
Bake me a cake as fast as you can,
Prick it and pat it and mark it with 'B',
And put it in the oven for Billy and me.

How did you feel about the activities?
Colour one of the faces.

People and their Jobs

Phonics and Spelling

er

A

1 Find these people in the picture:

paint**er** bak**er** wait**er** carpent**er**

2 Find these things in the picture:

lett**er** flow**er**s comput**er**s

B Circle the words you can read.
Read the words aloud.

| her | singer | farmer | butter | sister | letter |

C Circle the pictures that have **er** in the word.

er

A Trace the letters **er** with your finger.

 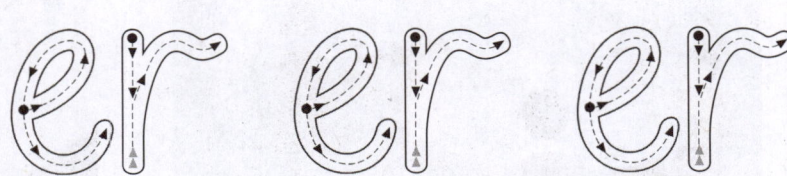

B Trace and copy the letters.

C Complete the words.

l___tt____   s___ ___pp ___ ___   l___dd ___ ___

  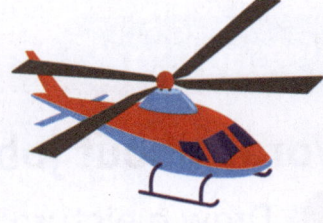

c___ ___k___ ___   h___mm ___ ___   h___licopt ___ ___

How did you feel about the activities?
Colour one of the faces.

Comprehension

What a job!

A   Look at the pictures and tell your partner what you can see.

1

This is Mrs Kadi. She is a teacher.

2

This is Mr Lal. He is a painter.

3

This is Ms Asher. She is a builder.

4

This is Mr Smith. He is a waiter.

B
1. Where is Mrs Kadi working?
2. Why is Mr Lal on a ladder?
3. What is Ms Asher's job?
4. Where is Mr Smith working?

C   Which job would you like to do and why?

Vocabulary

Words about jobs

A   Draw a picture for each word.

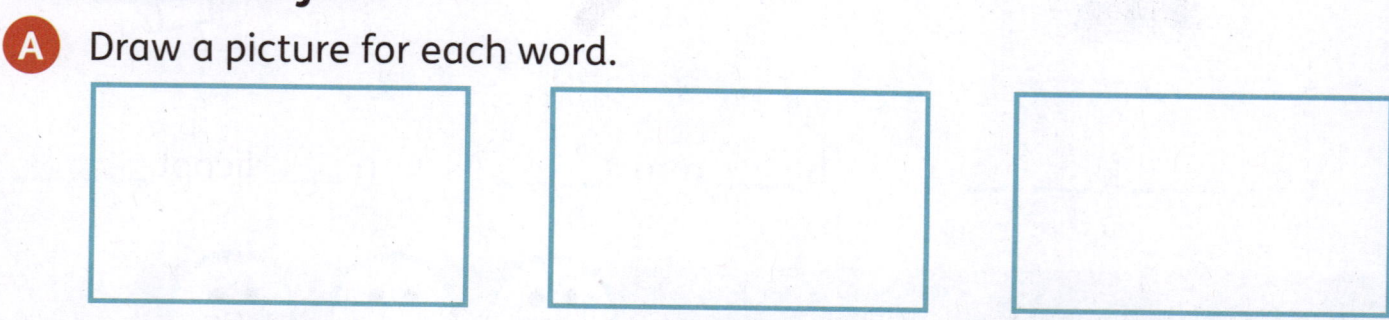

baker   singer   waiter

B   Match the pictures with the correct sentences.

1      I am a farmer.

2      I am a painter.

3      I am a builder.

Grammar and Punctuation

Answering a question

A   What would you like to be?
Write a sentence to answer.
For example: *I want to be a farmer.*

B   Say the rhyme and do some actions.

The painter in the street makes our shops bright,
Our shops bright, our shops bright,
The painter in the street makes our shops bright,
All day long.

The cleaner in the school makes our school clean,
Our school clean, our school clean,
The cleaner in the school makes our school clean,
All day long.

How did you feel about the activities?
Colour one of the faces.

BOOK B Phonics Check-up

1 Say the sound of each grapheme or digraph.

2 Read the words aloud.

3 Colour the star if you can read all the words.

Unit 1 ☆

j jet jump

v van vest

Unit 2 ☆

w wet wind

x fox box

Unit 3 ☆

y yam yes

z zip zero

Unit 4 ☆

qu quiz queen

th this think

Unit 5 ☆

sh shelf shell

ch chip chill

Unit 6 ☆

ng song bang

ai sail paint

Unit 7 ☆

ee feet sheet

oa float coat

Unit 8 ☆

oo soon spoon

oo fool tool

ar hard part

Unit 9 ☆

or port fork

ow now howl

Unit 10 ☆

oi soil point

ur hurt burnt

Unit 11 ☆

er singer trainer